D1061753

Party
IDEAS

WRITTEN BY
Hannah Dolan

MODELS BY
Nate Dias and
Jessica Farrell

Contents

I HOPE YOU ENJOY THIS BOOK!

Happy birthday!

Cake? Check. Balloons? Check. Gifts? Check. This lively kitchen scene can be only one thing: a minifigure birthday party. Hip hip hooray!

These kitchen cabinets are built into the wall

GIFT TABLE

The tiny kitchen table has a 3x3 plate tabletop and little round bricks for legs. It's the perfect size for minifigure presents!

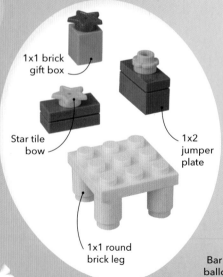

1x1 brick gift box

Star tile bow

1x2 jumper plate

1x1 round brick leg

Bar pieces are balloon strings

The kitchen clock attaches to a brick with side studs in the wall

Chocolate cake with cream and jelly filling

TOP TIP

Decorate your existing LEGO® houses or rooms to turn them into party scenes. It could be another kind of festivity, such as Halloween, Diwali, Purim, or Christmas.

HEY KITTY, IS IT YOUR PURR-DAY?

1x1 tile kitchen floor

Even the cat is having birthday treats!

9

Best wishes

Make LEGO greetings cards for any occasion! Wish your friends and family a happy birthday, say thank you, or tell them you love them.

GIFT CARD

Two quarter tiles make a pretty bow

Each card is built on one 6x8 plate

TOP TIP
You could build a layer of plates underneath, leaving some space to slip a handwritten note inside. Or add a bracket piece so the card can stand up.

IS THAT ANOTHER CARD FOR ME?

2x2 triangular tile

This could be a broken heart if you want to say sorry!

LOVE NOTE

Add 3-D elements, like this candle flame, using tiles with clips

1x2 jumper plate

1x1 half circle tiles make dripping icing

2x3 plates form the chocolate cake

BIRTHDAY CARD

YES, AND IT LOOKS LIKE YOUR HANDWRITING AGAIN!

The round tile pupils attach to jumper plates underneath

Two 2x2 macaroni tiles make a happy smile

CHEERFUL CARD

11

Anyone for cake?

No birthday is complete without a big slice of cake! Spread icing all over the top and sides and between the cake layers, then decorate it with bright sprinkles. Don't forget a candle to blow out, too.

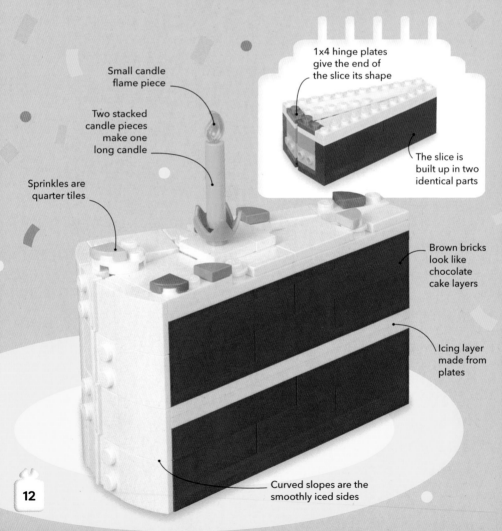

1x4 hinge plates give the end of the slice its shape

The slice is built up in two identical parts

Small candle flame piece

Two stacked candle pieces make one long candle

Sprinkles are quarter tiles

Brown bricks look like chocolate cake layers

Icing layer made from plates

Curved slopes are the smoothly iced sides

Cake stand

If you've gone to the trouble of building LEGO cakes, you'll need somewhere to present them at your party. This cake stand is perfect for displaying brick-built treats of any kind.

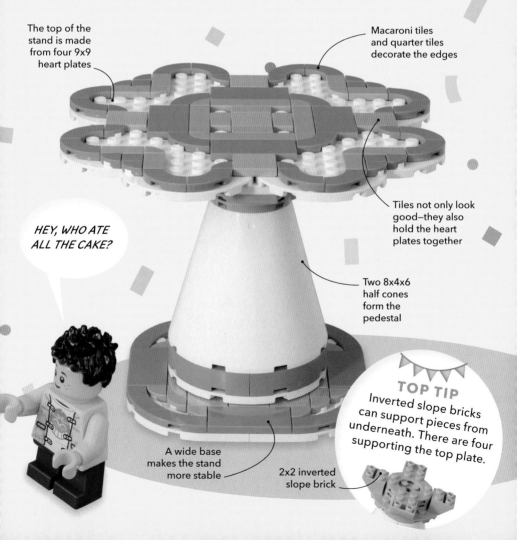

The top of the stand is made from four 9x9 heart plates

Macaroni tiles and quarter tiles decorate the edges

HEY, WHO ATE ALL THE CAKE?

Tiles not only look good—they also hold the heart plates together

Two 8x4x6 half cones form the pedestal

A wide base makes the stand more stable

2x2 inverted slope brick

TOP TIP
Inverted slope bricks can support pieces from underneath. There are four supporting the top plate.

Wacky presents

Give presents with personality by building a special box for your gift! Design a shape and size that suits your present, decide how you want to wrap it, then add a colorful ribbon and a bow.

TOP TIP
If you want the lid on your gift box to lift off easily, use a large plate or tile on top. If you use smaller pieces, your giftee can have fun dismantling it instead!

This part of the bow is made from stacked 2x2 wedge plates

RECTANGULAR PRESENT

These longer wedge plates are the ribbon ends

Build bricks with side studs into your box to attach the ribbon tiles to

SPECIAL PIECE

The middle of the big green bow is made from four inverted brackets. Fitted together, they make a square shape.

1x2/1x2 inverted bracket

Lots of tiny 1x1 cheese slopes form this fancy bow

SQUARE PRESENT

Use bricks and plates in alternating colors for wide stripes

PERFECT FIT

Make sure you leave plenty of hollow space inside your box if you want to fit a gift inside. You could measure your present before you start building to help you plan out your box.

GOOD THINGS COME IN SMALL PACKAGES.

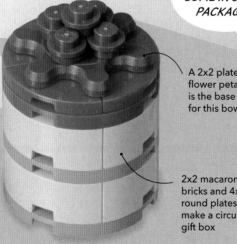

A 2x2 plate with flower petals is the base for this bow

2x2 macaroni bricks and 4x4 round plates make a circular gift box

CIRCULAR PRESENT

15

Beach party

The sun is shining, palm trees are swaying, and waves are lapping the shore—this is the perfect place to throw a laidback LEGO beach party!

These layered leaf pieces make a thatched palm roof

JUICE BAR

Goblets topped with 1x1 round plates and cherries

Bamboo counter made from 1x1 round bricks

A LEGO cake doesn't melt in the sun!

CAKE TABLE

The table colors match the wood on the juice bar

What else could you build for a beach party? How about lounge chairs, parasols, an ice-cream cart, or a beach bonfire? You could even make a calypso band with steel drums.

Palm tree leaf piece

Dinosaur tail tree trunk

PARTY PALM TREE

Presents in the shade of the tree

ALL RIGHT, I'LL PLAY YOUR SONG. DON'T GET CRABBY!

Spinning records are round jumper plates and star tiles

LET'S SHELL-ABRATE!

1x1 brick with three leaves

TURNTABLE

17

Find that minifigure!

Help your friends come out of their shells with this fun guessing game! You could build any identical shapes—just leave a minifigure-sized space inside.

2x2 inverted slope turtle tail

HOW TO PLAY

1 Place a minifigure under one of the turtle shells.

2 Mix up the shells in front of your friends—the faster, the better!

3 Line up the shells, then ask your friends to guess which shell the minifigure is hiding under.

This hollow space is six studs long and four studs wide

Printed eye tiles attach to sideways-facing studs

IT'S TURTLEY DARK UNDER THERE!

2x2 wedge slope pieces make the shell more rounded

18

Party champion

And the winner is ... Award a LEGO trophy to any deserving party guests. It could be a glittering gold cup, a statue, or your own design themed around the game or competition you're awarding the prize for.

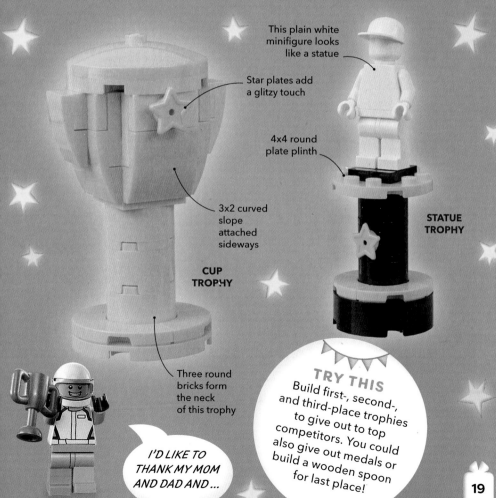

This plain white minifigure looks like a statue

Star plates add a glitzy touch

4x4 round plate plinth

STATUE TROPHY

3x2 curved slope attached sideways

CUP TROPHY

Three round bricks form the neck of this trophy

I'D LIKE TO THANK MY MOM AND DAD AND ...

TRY THIS
Build first-, second-, and third-place trophies to give out to top competitors. You could also give out medals or build a wooden spoon for last place!

19

Rally car racers

Move your party up a gear with this super-speedy racing game. First, build a start line, ramps and obstacles, and a rally car of your own design, then start your engines!

HOW TO PLAY

1 Line up your LEGO rally cars on the launching ramp.

2 Ready, set, race! Whizz around the racetrack, tackling any jumps and obstacles.

3 The first rally car to cross the finish line is the winner. You could even hand the winner a LEGO trophy! Find some build ideas on page 19.

This checkered design is made from a lot of 1x1 bricks

Wide 2x6 plates at the base make the model more stable

YOU'VE WON BY MILES!

Your rally car can be any style and color—just don't forget the wheels!

RALLY CARS

Use 2x2 curved slopes to make the end of the ramp curved

Tiles make a smooth surface for the rally cars to roll off

LAUNCHING RAMP

Just three pieces make a traffic cone obstacle

This is one long 2x16 plate, but you can also use lots of smaller plates

1x2 slope bricks support the hinge plates from underneath

2x2 hinge plates hold the ramp at an angle

I'M ALWAYS READY TO RACE!

START/ FINISH LINE

Alice's tea party

This must be one of the most famous tea parties ever! Recreate this quirky scene from *Alice's Adventures in Wonderland* or any other parties from books or movies.

2x1 curved slopes secure the branches

I'M LATE FOR AN IMPORTANT DATE!

Strawberry tart tiles on a 2x2 plate

Toadstool is a 2x2 radar dish and 1x1 cone

Checkered table runner made from 1x1 tiles

AFTERNOON TEA

Alice, the Dormouse, and the
March Hare are having tea
with the Mad Hatter. The
enormous teapot should
hold enough tea for
endless cups all afternoon.

The arm on this
1x2 plate is the
teapot's spout

Inverted dome
teapot base

1x1 rounded
plate with
handle

THIS IS AN
UNBIRTHDAY
PARTY.

Build your own
top hat from
a round brick,
plates, and tiles

Trees in an
imaginary place
can be any
color you like

Chair back is a
1x2 plate with
angled bar
handles

23

Spin to win

Challenge your friends to be the first to build a minifigure, body part by body part, with this head (and body) spinning party game!

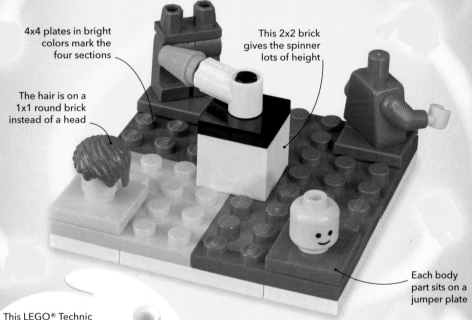

4x4 plates in bright colors mark the four sections

This 2x2 brick gives the spinner lots of height

The hair is on a 1x1 round brick instead of a head

Each body part sits on a jumper plate

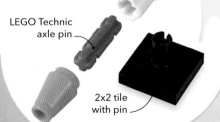

This LEGO® Technic connector spins on the pin below

LEGO Technic axle pin

2x2 tile with pin

HOW TO PLAY

1 Gather some minifigures—one for each player—and take them apart so they're in four parts.

2 Take turns to spin the dial. Each player should gradually build up each part of the minifigure.

3 The winner is the player who finishes their minifigure first.

Party balloons

Build balloons with personality to welcome people to your party. These adorable inflatables each have their own unique look.

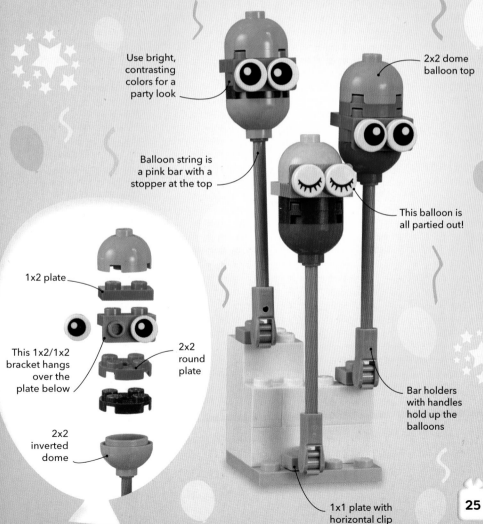

Use bright, contrasting colors for a party look

2x2 dome balloon top

Balloon string is a pink bar with a stopper at the top

This balloon is all partied out!

1x2 plate

This 1x2/1x2 bracket hangs over the plate below

2x2 round plate

2x2 inverted dome

Bar holders with handles hold up the balloons

1x1 plate with horizontal clip

Jungle
big band

These animals aren't just monkeying around. They're a jamming jungle band of musicians, ready to make some serious noise at any party!

1x1 double curved slope monkey ears

TRY THIS
Your jungle band can consist of any animals and instruments you like. Build a snake playing a saxophone, a sloth on a harp, a lion on a cello, or a baboon on a bassoon!

Rotund 2x2 round tile tummy

Piano keys are six 1x2 grille plates

These plant plates attach to bracket pieces built into the piano

LET'S GO BANANAS!

2x2 round brick with a tile on top

This drum stand is a telescope piece

Tile with pin is the bass drum base

Long arms made from 1x3x2 curved arches

These satellite dishes are the crash cymbal

Tapping toes are 1x2 rounded plates

Bar piece drum stick

Leafy jungle greenery

All parts of the drum fit onto this 4x6 base plate

The center of the bass drum is a 4x4 round brick with pin holes

Bright bunting

Jazz up your party venue by hanging up this brick-built bunting. Each flag is made from a 4x4 plate. Add smaller pieces to each one to make your own designs.

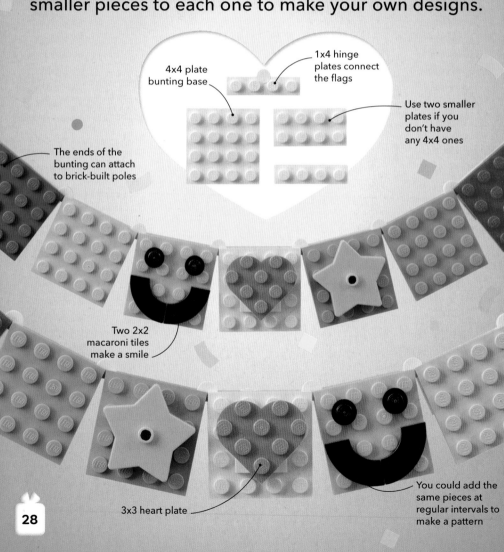

4x4 plate bunting base

1x4 hinge plates connect the flags

Use two smaller plates if you don't have any 4x4 ones

The ends of the bunting can attach to brick-built poles

Two 2x2 macaroni tiles make a smile

3x3 heart plate

You could add the same pieces at regular intervals to make a pattern

The star drops hang from the hole of a 2x3 plate

An extra layer of tiles here hides the ends of the strings

Star drops

Twinkle twinkle little star, make your party sparkle wherever you are! Use LEGO string to hang up friendly stars, colorful circles, or wintry snowflakes.

This icy snowflake is one piece

1x1 cones add extra sparkle

THESE STAR DROPS ARE TUTU SWEET.

Even simple 2x2 boat studs can make shimmering star drops

The hole in the middle of this star plate looks like a mouth!

SPECIAL PIECE

This LEGO string has tiny 1x1 round plates at either end that can attach to other pieces.

Birthday numbers

Let everyone at your birthday party know exactly how old you're turning by building your age in LEGO pieces. Create two of these numbers if you've reached double figures!

2x1 slope brick

YOU'RE THE ONLY ONE FOR ME!

Transparent bricks support parts of the numbers

These bricks and plates are "offset" to make a curved shape

TOP TIP
Think of where the heaviest or biggest part of a number is and build in wider or heavier pieces in other places to balance it out, so your number doesn't topple over.

This 1x4 brick makes a wide base for balance

Lunar New Year

Throw a light-filled festivity to celebrate the first new moon of the lunar calendar. Build hanging lanterns, fireworks, and a dancing dragon!

HAPPY LUNAR NEW YEAR!

String with climbing grips

HANGING LANTERNS

This lamppost base is all one piece

TOP TIP
These lanterns all hang from tiles with clips, but yours could hang from pieces with hooks or rings instead. You can attach your lanterns to any LEGO string or bar piece.

1x1 round brick with bamboo leaves

BAMBOO PLANTS

FIREWORKS

1x1 cone firework head

Bar piece fits into a round brick with an open stud

This axle pin holds the two domes together

1x1 tile with vertical clip

2x2 dome

THESE CELEBRATIONS DO DRAG-ON!

1x2 bricks with side studs hold the eyes and horns

Orange leaf plates look like fiery dragon horns

1x2/1x2 bracket nostrils

Two grille plates make lots of teeth!

1x1 cheese slope back spikes

NEW YEAR DRAGON

Pick 'n' mix

Colorful candies add a sweet touch to a party scene. You can use any shape, color, or style for your pick 'n' mix selection. You could also build a bag or bowl to serve them in.

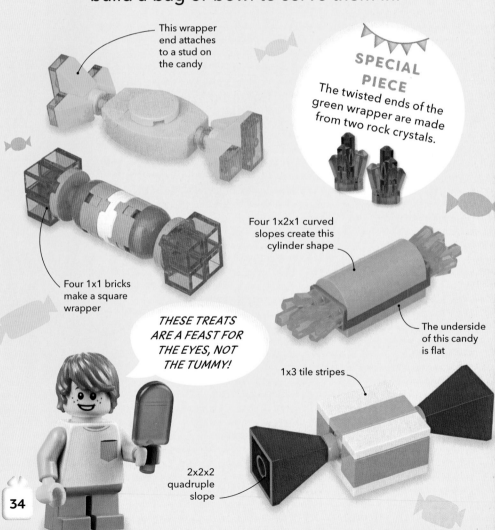

This wrapper end attaches to a stud on the candy

SPECIAL PIECE
The twisted ends of the green wrapper are made from two rock crystals.

Four 1x1 bricks make a square wrapper

Four 1x2x1 curved slopes create this cylinder shape

The underside of this candy is flat

THESE TREATS ARE A FEAST FOR THE EYES, NOT THE TUMMY!

1x3 tile stripes

2x2x2 quadruple slope

Charming cupcakes

Chocolate, strawberry, or vanilla? Use your LEGO® pieces to whip up fluffy cupcakes in any flavor you like, then top them with small tiles for decoration.

Quarter tile sprinkle

Candle holder is a minifigure crown

Use heart tiles for a sprinkle of love!

Thick chocolate icing made from small bricks and plates

Transparent tiles look like shiny pieces of candy

1x2 brick with two side studs

Each side is made from small plates and a brick

Flower
decorations

Bring some floral fun to your party table by decorating it with colorful plants and flowers. Take inspiration from nature or dream up imaginary species.

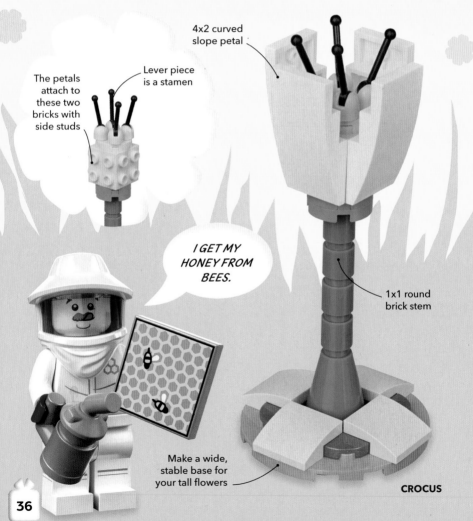

4x2 curved slope petal

The petals attach to these two bricks with side studs

Lever piece is a stamen

I GET MY HONEY FROM BEES.

1x1 round brick stem

Make a wide, stable base for your tall flowers

CROCUS

36

The center of this flower is a 2x2 radar dish

3x1 curved slope petal

These 4x3 leaf pieces fit onto the stem

MICHAELMAS DAISY

Upside-down 2x2 round plate with six petals

2x2 boat stud stamen

Four 2x4 double curved slopes make a flower pot

I GET MY HONEY FROM THE SUPERMARKET!

Stem is three stacked minifigure candles

Leave roots so more flowers can grow!

FORGET-ME-NOT

37

Party placeholders

Build LEGO placeholders to let everyone know where to sit at your party table. These three different designs can all hold cards for your guests' names.

A name card can rest on this 1x2x1 panel

Decorate your placeholders to suit the theme of your party

Bar holders with clips hold up the balloons

An inverted slope brick here holds the card holder at an angle

NOW I JUST NEED TO DECIDE WHO TO PUT NEXT TO WHOM!

1x2 plate with bar

Louis

A name card can slot in between four well-placed 1x1 round plates

2x4 brick base

Fun-loving foods

These partying portions of your five-a-day will fit right in at any kitchen disco! Build your favorite fruits and vegetables, then add eyes and limbs to bring them to life.

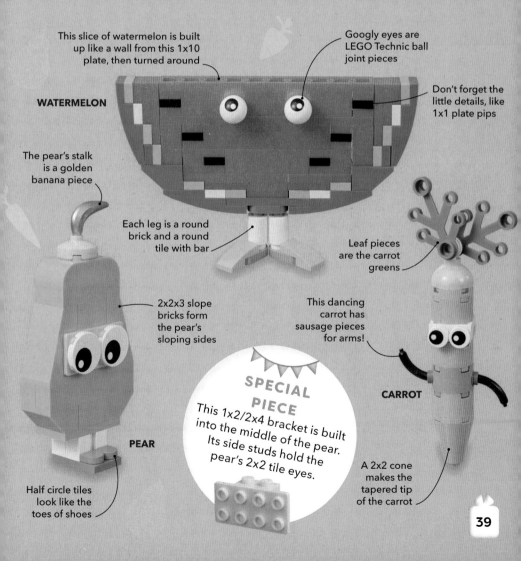

This slice of watermelon is built up like a wall from this 1x10 plate, then turned around

Googly eyes are LEGO Technic ball joint pieces

WATERMELON

Don't forget the little details, like 1x1 plate pips

The pear's stalk is a golden banana piece

Each leg is a round brick and a round tile with bar

Leaf pieces are the carrot greens

2x2x3 slope bricks form the pear's sloping sides

This dancing carrot has sausage pieces for arms!

SPECIAL PIECE
This 1x2/2x4 bracket is built into the middle of the pear. Its side studs hold the pear's 2x2 tile eyes.

PEAR

CARROT

Half circle tiles look like the toes of shoes

A 2x2 cone makes the tapered tip of the carrot

39

Stars of the stage

Get your party jumping with a minifigure pop performance! Build your band a stage with flashing lights, a booming sound system, and a dance floor to throw some serious shapes on.

HELLO, PARTY PEOPLE!

PSST ... IS IT TIME FOR MY SOLO?

SPECIAL PIECE

This 2x2x10 triangular girder is ideal for stage rigging. Two of these pieces hold up the tall sides of the stage. You could also build your own stage rigging using bricks.

Hidden treasures

Build LEGO treasures, then hide them for your friends to find at your party! Create glistening jewels, gold doubloons, and a wooden chest for a pirate-themed treasure hunt.

I'VE HIDDEN TREASURE AROUND THE ROOM, ME HEARTY.

TRY THIS
It's not only pirates who look for hidden treasure! You could build colorful eggs for an Easter Bunny-themed hunt or creepy critters for a Halloween-themed one.

2x1x1 curved slopes make these rounded edges

These brown pieces are a wooden handle

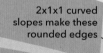

Four 1x4 double curved slopes form the lid

Yellow pieces look like golden details

TREASURE CHEST

The center of each jewel is a 1x6 plate

These precious jewels are all diamond shapes

JEWELS

2x1 slope brick

2x1 inverted slope bricks make this tapered part

HOW TO PLAY

1 Hide your treasures in various places around your party venue.

2 Find that treasure! Challenge your friends to hunt for as many LEGO treasures as they can.

3 The winner is the partygoer who has found the most booty! Will they share it with their friends?

AYE AYE, CAPTAIN! I'LL SPY THEM OUT.

You could add orange or brown pieces for a rustier look!

Small plates and bricks fill the center of the coin

GOLD COINS

Curved slope edges

Egg splat

Make your party eggs-tra special with an egg and spoon race! This LEGO egg can break if it falls off your spoon. Will you whisk it?

The inside of the egg is hollow

1x1 brick with side studs

Layers of plates create the egg's shell

THIS PARTY IDEA IS NO YOLK!

CRACKED IT

Just like the real thing, when this LEGO egg cracks open, egg whites and yolk spill out!

1x1 plate egg white

Only four studs connect to the other half of the egg so it opens easily

Candle bowling

Don't blow out your birthday candles—bowl them over!
Build these candle pins and see how many you can
knock down. You may even get a birthday strike!

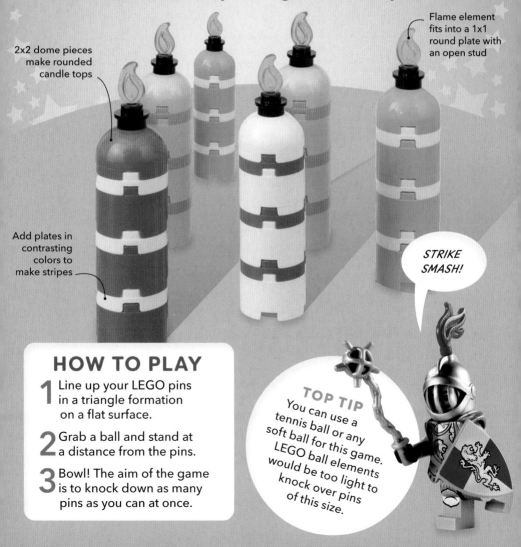

2x2 dome pieces
make rounded
candle tops

Flame element
fits into a 1x1
round plate with
an open stud

Add plates in
contrasting
colors to
make stripes

*STRIKE
SMASH!*

HOW TO PLAY

1 Line up your LEGO pins
in a triangle formation
on a flat surface.

2 Grab a ball and stand at
a distance from the pins.

3 Bowl! The aim of the game
is to knock down as many
pins as you can at once.

TOP TIP
You can use a
tennis ball or any
soft ball for this game.
LEGO ball elements
would be too light to
knock over pins
of this size.

Photo booth fun

Strike the picture-perfect party pose with these silly photo booth props! Sport a curly moustache, throw on some super-cool shades, or pucker up with a pout.

1x1 cheese slopes make curly tips

Slope bricks form the handlebar shape

Inverted slope pieces here leave space for a mouth

HANDLEBAR MOUSTACHE

This transparent bar is the prop handle

HOLD THAT POSE!

The bar has a 1x2 plate at the end so it can be built into the prop

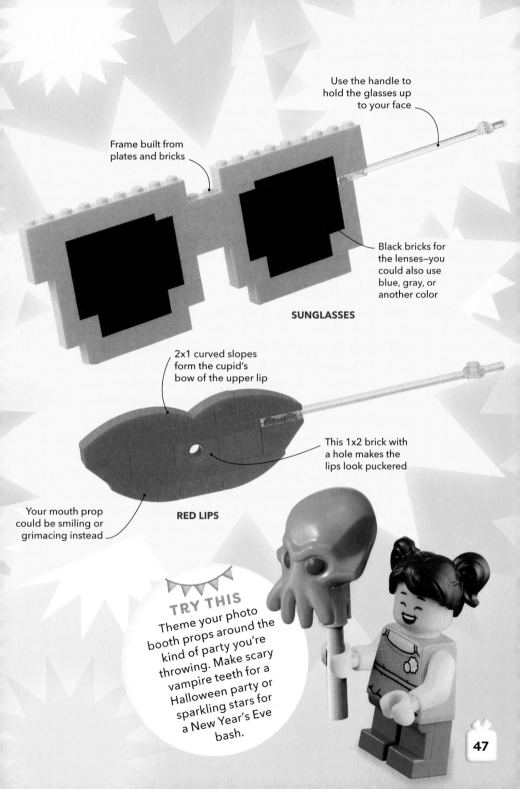

Use the handle to hold the glasses up to your face

Frame built from plates and bricks

Black bricks for the lenses—you could also use blue, gray, or another color

SUNGLASSES

2x1 curved slopes form the cupid's bow of the upper lip

This 1x2 brick with a hole makes the lips look puckered

Your mouth prop could be smiling or grimacing instead

RED LIPS

TRY THIS

Theme your photo booth props around the kind of party you're throwing. Make scary vampire teeth for a Halloween party or sparkling stars for a New Year's Eve bash.

Party like a pirate

When pirates find a chest brimming with treasure, there's only one thing to do ... throw a bouncing buccaneer bash on a desert island beach. Arrrr!

This dinosaur tail piece makes a bendy palm tree trunk

Hidden pins hold the sections of the trunk together

WAIT, DOES ANYONE REMEMBER WHERE WE LEFT OUR SHIP?

Dark tan plates are wet sand

Aqua round tiles look like sea foam

MY FAVORITE TYPE OF MUSIC IS ARRRR AND B.

TRY THIS

What other imaginary party scenarios can you dream up? You could create a snowy party thrown by Santa's elves on Christmas Eve or a fantastical fairy party deep in the forest.

Palm tree leaves clip onto a special tree top piece with four prongs

Perhaps the pirates found the treasure in this hollow cave

2x2 slope bricks are sand drifts

Build a beach bonfire for your pirates to toast marshmallows on!

MY FAVORITE MUSICAL NOTE IS THE HIGH C.

49

Cracker
surprise

Grab a friend and pull apart this brick-built cracker to find out what's inside— SNAP! It's filled with colorful tile confetti.

This shape fits into a space on the other half of the cracker

Quarter tile confetti—what else could you fill a cracker with?

Use plates and bricks in contrasting colors to make stripes

Cracker ends are 4x4x2 cones with axle holes

This axle pin threads through one side of the cracker

2x4x2 half cylinder with cutout sides

Musical
microphone

This life-size microphone will bring some karaoke fun to your party. What will you sing? It even has an on-off switch in case anyone's hogging it too much!

Musical notes made from small tiles

Build a large round grille to sing into

Tile and cheese slope power switch

Stacked 4x4 round bricks

1x1 brick with two side studs

Layers of small plates make these rounded side panels

DO DO DO ... I'VE FORGOTTEN THE WORDS!

Let's go fishing!

Your party guests will reely have fun with this fiddly fishing game! Build a fishing rod with a hook and lots of fish. Who will make the catch of the day?

I'M HOOKED ON THIS GAME!

HOW TO PLAY

1 Place all your fish in one place or hide them in various spots around your party venue.

2 Challenge players to hook as many fish as they can with their rods—the bigger, the better!

SPECIAL PIECE

This handy hookable ring piece is a minifigure life buoy or flotation ring. It has one stud so it can attach to other pieces.

Long 1x10 plate

This blue piece is a bracket with side studs

FISHING ROD

Spinning reel and handle

This LEGO chain has a stud at each end

1x1 tile eye attached sideways

This 2x1 curved slope looks like an upturned mouth

The tail fin is made from two 2x1 slope bricks

LARGE FISH

1x3 tow ball hook

Six slope bricks form this little fish

1x4 plate center

SMALL FISH

Party crown

Build some magnificent headwear to show everyone who's party royalty! This small crown is perfect for teddy bears or dolls at a birthday tea party.

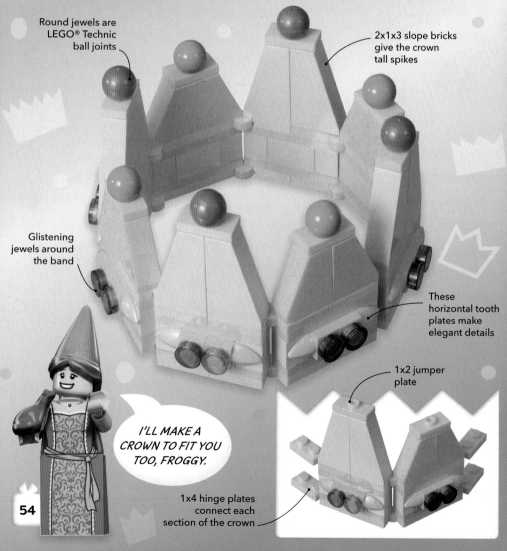

Round jewels are LEGO® Technic ball joints

2x1x3 slope bricks give the crown tall spikes

Glistening jewels around the band

These horizontal tooth plates make elegant details

1x2 jumper plate

I'LL MAKE A CROWN TO FIT YOU TOO, FROGGY.

1x4 hinge plates connect each section of the crown

Challenge chest

Are you ready for a challenge? Build this intriguing box and fill it with awesome LEGO building challenges for you and your friends to complete at your party.

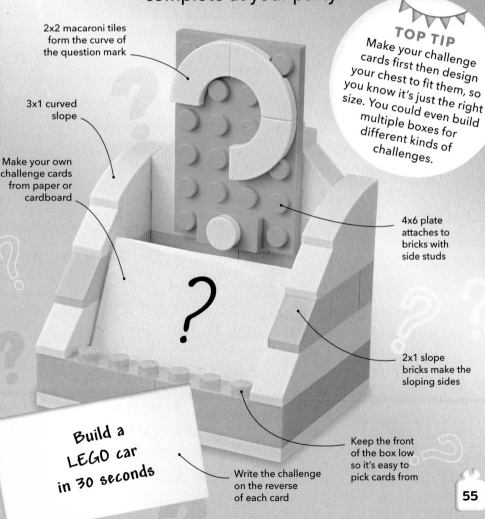

2x2 macaroni tiles form the curve of the question mark

3x1 curved slope

Make your own challenge cards from paper or cardboard

TOP TIP
Make your challenge cards first then design your chest to fit them, so you know it's just the right size. You could even build multiple boxes for different kinds of challenges.

4x6 plate attaches to bricks with side studs

2x1 slope bricks make the sloping sides

Build a LEGO car in 30 seconds

Write the challenge on the reverse of each card

Keep the front of the box low so it's easy to pick cards from

Pool party

Have your minifigures throw on their swimming trunks ... because you're throwing them a splash-tastic pool party! Build a swimming pool and water slide, floats, lounge chairs, and a bubbling hot tub.

2x2 curved slope back rest

2x3 flag tile

Arm rests are nozzle pieces

Glistening water is transparent blue tiles and plates

LOUNGE CHAIRS

Hot tub bubbles are a four-scoop ice-cream piece

These palisade bricks look like wooden panels

HOT TUB

THE HOT TUB IS SWITCHED OFF. WHY ARE THERE BUBBLES?

Tallest tower

Topple the competition with this tower-building game! Challenge your party guests to build tall towers to music. Will yours be as tall as you?

Tall pieces like this 1x2x5 brick will help you reach great heights quickly!

Add wide bricks to make it stable

GAME RULES

1 Turn on your favorite party tunes and ask your guests to build tall towers to the music.

2 Turn off the tunes. When the music stops, the building stops!

3 Take a look at everyone's towers and declare the tallest one the winner.

ERM, WHERE'S THE STAIRCASE?

Sparkly disco balls

Entice your party guests to the dance floor with these glittering disco balls! They can hang from the ceiling and light up the room.

A hidden axle pin here joins this LEGO Technic connector to the ball

Thread string through this hole to hang the ball up

There's one 4x4 round plate with hole on each side

The underside will be seen from the dance floor

TOP TIP
Use bricks with side studs so you can attach one 4x4 plate to each side.

Lots of small transparent pieces reflect the light

Perfect
picture frames

Display your most memorable party moments in a brick-built picture frame! This design has a birthday theme, but the same basic model could work with any theme you choose.

You can add plates or tiles to these 1x2/1x2 brackets

The photo rests on stacked 1x4 bricks

TOP TIP
Building a wide base for your picture frame allows you to decorate it with smaller models at the front. It also makes the picture frame more stable so it won't fall over.

BASIC FRAME

The base is made from two 4x6 plates

QUICK! I CANT HOLD MY SMILE FOR MUCH LONGER.

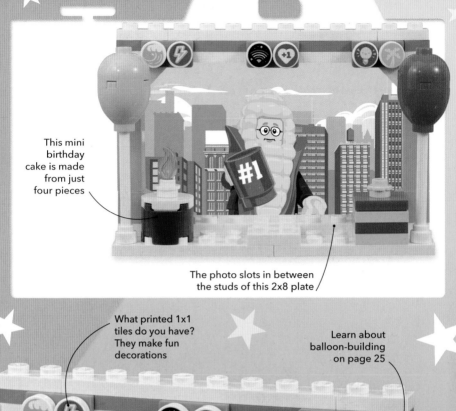

This mini birthday cake is made from just four pieces

The photo slots in between the studs of this 2x8 plate

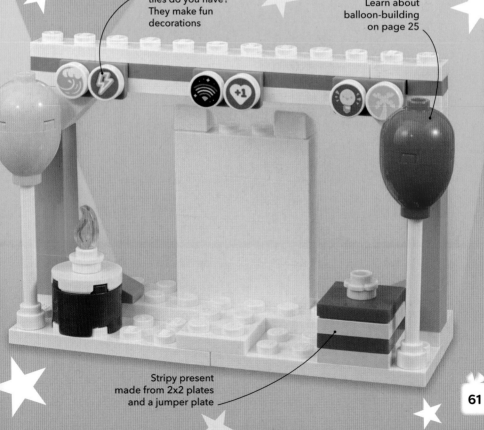

What printed 1x1 tiles do you have? They make fun decorations

Learn about balloon-building on page 25

Stripy present made from 2x2 plates and a jumper plate

61

Brick bingo

YOU CAN BORROW MY TEDDY, BUT I WANT HIM BACK AFTERWARD.

Eyes down ... Create bingo boards and fill them with your favorite small pieces and minifigure accessories. Which party guest will be the first to shout "BINGO!"?

This board has a checkered design but yours could be multiple colors

BUILD A BOARD

This square bingo board is built on a 16x16 base plate, with smaller tiles and plates on top.

2x2 round plates replace the accessory pieces when they're called

TOP TIP

If you have two of each accessory, put one in a bag for the bingo caller to pick from. If not, write down the name of each accessory or piece and put the names in the bag instead.

Any small pieces in your collection will work

2x2 jumper plate

RULES

1 Give out bingo boards to all players, making sure the boards have pieces on every square.

2 Make one player the bingo caller, who selects pieces from a bag. Ask them to pick one piece without looking.

3 Whichever player has the matching piece on their board can replace it with a plate.

4 The first player to get one line of plates is the first winner! After that, play for two lines and then a full house.

ONE LINE

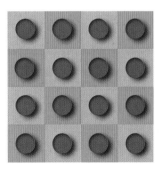

FULL HOUSE

Rocket-fueled fun

How do aliens like to party? Build them a bash that's literally out of this world! This one features a roaring rocket, a moon-dust dance floor, and a dazzling disco moon buggy.

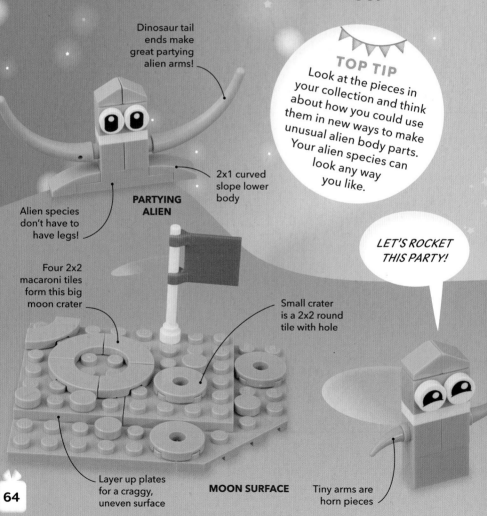

Dinosaur tail ends make great partying alien arms!

TOP TIP
Look at the pieces in your collection and think about how you could use them in new ways to make unusual alien body parts. Your alien species can look any way you like.

2x1 curved slope lower body

PARTYING ALIEN

Alien species don't have to have legs!

LET'S ROCKET THIS PARTY!

Four 2x2 macaroni tiles form this big moon crater

Small crater is a 2x2 round tile with hole

Layer up plates for a craggy, uneven surface

MOON SURFACE

Tiny arms are horn pieces

ROCKET SHIP

Two cheese slopes are the rocket's nose cone

2x2 tile windows

Disco lights are the backs of transparent round plates

This is the back of a 4x4 plate

Satellite dish sound system

2x1 curved slope

2x1 inverted brick tail fin

1x2 plate with handle

I TAUGHT THEM TO MOONWALK.

DISCO MOON BUGGY

Tiles with vertical clips attach the jazzy headlights to the car

2x10 plate chassis base

Pumpkin shy

Roll up, roll up ... Take aim and try to knock pumpkins from their perches in this classic game, which is often played at fairs and circuses.

These plates with rails allow the shooter to move along the front wall

The rails on the shooter fit into these 1x4 bricks with grooves

TAKE AIM AND WIN THIS TEDDY!

SPECIAL PIECE
This 1x4 brick is called a spring shooter. It's specially designed to hold and fire LEGO projectiles.

The shooter holds three projectiles

I WANT ANOTHER GO!

HEY, WATCH IT!

HOW TO PLAY

1 Load up the shooter with three projectile arrows.

2 Aim the shooter at a pumpkin and FIRE! Did you hit it? Aim for another pumpkin if you did.

3 Award different prizes for knocking off one, two, or three pumpkins.

Pumpkins sit on top of smooth round tiles so they can be knocked off

Jazz up the plinths with small star tiles

Use smooth tiles here so the shooter can slide along

Colorful transparent tiles look like lights

67

Great goody bags

It's the end of your party, but the LEGO® fun doesn't have to stop there. Build some amazing mini builds for your guests to take home in their goody bags.

Transparent 2x2 slope brick windshield

2x6 plate chassis

TRUCK

TOP TIP

Buy or make your goody bags first so you can figure out just how mini your mini builds should be! Theme the builds around your party or personalize them to your guests.

Lever pieces make good antennae!

Vertical tooth plates built into the body

ALIEN

2x2 inverted
dome flower

This 1x1
plate fits in
the middle
of the dome

**FLOWER
POT**

2x2 round
brick pot

1x2 tile
beak

DUCK

Two 2x1 slope
bricks make
a tiny roof

Blue tail plumage
is a 2x1 curved
slope

Mini hedge is
stacked 1x1
round plates

2x6 plate
garden lawn

HOUSE

*I COME ONLY FOR
THE GOODY BAGS!*

Editor Nicole Reynolds
Designer James McKeag
Senior Production Editor Jennifer Murray
Senior Production Controller
Lloyd Robertson
Managing Editor Paula Regan
Managing Art Editor Jo Connor
Publishing Director Mark Searle
Model Photography Gary Ombler

Packaged for DK by Plum Jam
Editor Hannah Dolan **Designer** Guy Harvey

Models designed and created by
Nate Dias and Jessica Farrell

Additional balloon model on page 25
designed and created by Emily Corl

Dorling Kindersley would like to thank:
Randi Sørensen, Heidi K. Jensen, Paul
Hansford, Martin Leighton Lindhardt, Nina
Koopmann, Charlotte Neidhardt, and
Susan Due at the LEGO Group; and
Jennette ElNaggar for proofreading.

First American Edition, 2022
Published in the United States by
DK Publishing
1450 Broadway, Suite 801,
New York, NY 10018

Page design copyright ©2022 Dorling
Kindersley Limited
DK, a Division of Penguin Random House LLC
22 23 24 25 26 10 9 8 7 6 5 4 3 2 1

MIX
Paper from
responsible sources
FSC™ C018179

This book was made with
Forest Stewardship Council™
certified paper—one small
step in DK's commitment to
a sustainable future.

Meet the creators

NATE DIAS
A science teacher by
day and a LEGO® master
builder by night, Nate won
the first-ever series of
LEGO® *Masters* on TV. He particularly
likes building animals, so the jungle big
band on page 26 is his favorite model.

JESSICA FARRELL
Jessica is a professional
brick artist from Ireland.
Her favorite builds in
the book are the pick
'n' mix candies on page 34. She
liked designing the colorful candy
wrappers from different pieces.